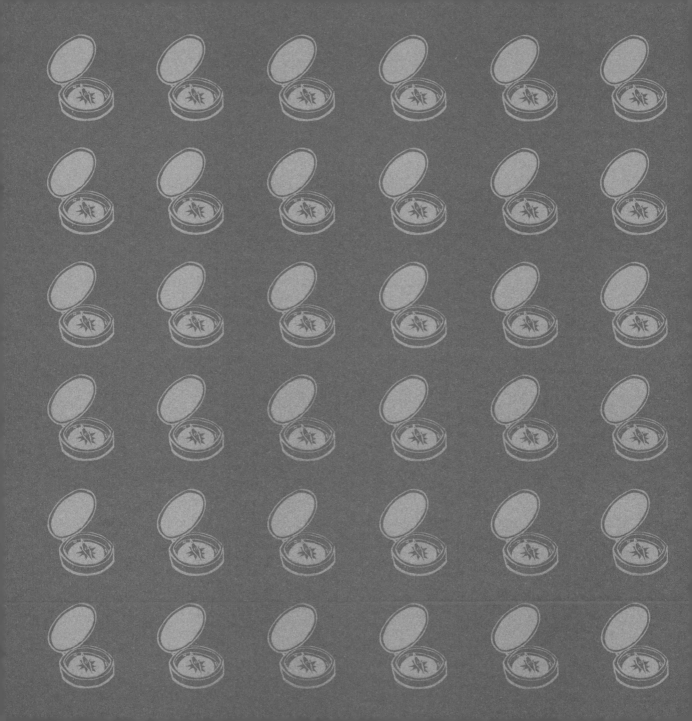

ORDINARY
PEOPLE
CHANGE
the
WORLD

I am Albert Einstein

BRAD MELTZER

illustrated by Christopher Eliopoulos

DIAL BOOKS FOR YOUNG READERS an imprint of Penguin Group (USA) LLC

I am **Albert Einstein**.

Ever been called weird? Or different?
That's what they thought I was.
On the day I was born, my mom was actually scared since she'd never seen a baby with such a giant head.

It didn't get easier.
I did things my own way. In my own time.
I didn't speak until I was three years old.
And when I did, my speech was so odd,
our maid used to call me . . .

Some say I took longer to speak because I didn't think in words. I thought in pictures.

Even when I did speak, I'd practice each sentence in my head, silently moving my lips and whispering to myself, until I had every word right.

When I was little, my cousins ran around and played games outside. I liked playing alone. I did puzzles, fed the pigeons, or just watched my toy boat sail in a water pail.
When they saw me, other people called me . . .

But the biggest moment in my young life came when
I was four or five years old and sick in bed.
To cheer me up, my father brought me a compass.

I was fascinated by how the compass worked. No matter which way my father turned it, its needle always pointed north.

Nothing touched
the needle, but somehow
the compass "knew" where to point.
Like it was guided by an invisible
force.
Right there, I could feel it:
There was something behind
things, something deeply hidden.

The world . . . the stars . . .
even outer space with all its
planets . . .
   The whole universe had its
own order.
   That compass made a deep
and lasting impression on me.

It showed me that life
has mystery. The universe
has mystery.
   And it made me curious.
Why did the universe
behave the way it did?

By the time I was nine years old, I would make complex structures with my blocks . . .

. . . and tall houses of cards.

It took persistence. And patience.

But I never gave up.

My sister would watch as I'd build them fourteen stories high.

IT'S GONNA FALL.

I'd even see the structure in music as I played my favorite instrument—the one that always helped me think: the violin.

Today, people say I was a genius.
But back then, teachers thought
I was a daydreamer.
One even told me . . .

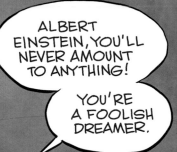

But there's nothing foolish about dreaming big and being curious.

When I was in sixth grade, on Thursday nights, a medical student would come to our house for dinner.

Like the compass, that geometry book changed my life.

By the time I was twelve, I was doing all different kinds of math, like geometry and algebra.

By fifteen, I was onto something called calculus.

Soon after, I mastered the entire math curriculum.

I never stopped thinking about how things work.

As I got older, I even replaced my toy sailboat with a real one.

When the wind stopped blowing, I scribbled notes in my notepad.

When it picked up again, I continued sailing.

My thinking—and curious nature—eventually led me to the patent office in Bern, Switzerland.
My job was to examine new inventions.

But sometimes, I'd start thinking about my own scientific theories. Whenever my boss walked by, I'd hide my ideas in my desk drawer.

But even I didn't know I was on the verge
of my greatest breakthrough.

I was twenty-eight years old, just sitting at work as the thought occurred to me.

When a person falls—like a man falling off a roof—he doesn't feel his own weight.

Close your eyes. You can picture it too.

As the man falls, if he opens his pockets, everything inside floats there next to him.

That may sound weird . . . or different . . . but for me,
it was the happiest thought of my life.

Why?

Because it sparked an idea that helped me link motion
with gravity. (Gravity is the force in the universe that keeps
us from floating away.)

It took me eight years of hard work—eight years of asking
hard questions—to figure it out. But I did.

From there, I began to question ideas that most other scientists thought were true.
I didn't agree with what most people believed.
In the beginning, other scientists wouldn't listen.

Sometimes it's hard to get people to go along with you—especially when you discover something new. But I promise you, if you keep at it . . .

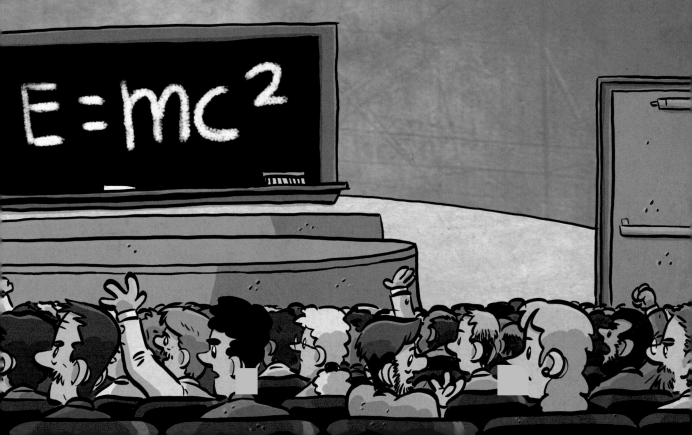

It'll be worth it.

In my life, I was always thinking.
Always asking questions.
But the most important one I asked was:
Why?

Never stop asking "Why?"
Never stop trying to figure out how the world works.
And never lose that feeling of excitement as you try
to find the answer.

Curiosity is one of the most powerful forces of nature.
It can take you places no one's ever been,
and let you do things no one's ever done.
Will that make you weird? Or different?
Who cares if it does?
Every single one of us is different.
No one on this planet is just like you.

DREAM

Being different is what makes you special.
So find what you love.
Learn everything you can about it.
And share the best parts with anyone
who will listen.
You never know who you'll inspire.

I am Albert Einstein.
I will never stop being curious.
And I hope you won't either.

The more questions you ask, the more answers you'll find.
And the more beauty you'll uncover in the universe.

"*The important thing is not to stop questioning. Curiosity has its own reason for existing. One cannot help but be in awe when he contemplates the mysteries of eternity, of life, of the marvelous structure of reality.*"

—ALBERT EINSTEIN

Albert as a boy with
his sister, Maja

Albert the sailor

Timeline

MARCH 14, 1877
Born in Ulm, Germany

1896
Enrolled in Zurich
Polytechnic at age 17

1900
Received teaching
diploma

1905
Received PhD from
University of Zurich

1908
Began college-level
teaching

**Albert
on a bicycle**

**This famous photo of
Albert was taken on his
72nd birthday**

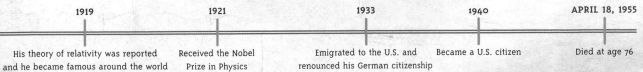

1919	1921	1933	1940	APRIL 18, 1955
His theory of relativity was reported and he became famous around the world	Received the Nobel Prize in Physics	Emigrated to the U.S. and renounced his German citizenship	Became a U.S. citizen	Died at age 76

··

For Cori,
the girl who was different than everyone else,
the girl who was smarter than everyone else,
and the girl who made my life by bringing order to my universe
—B.M

For my father, Christo,
my first hero and the person who didn't flinch when
I said I wanted to grow up to be a cartoonist
—C.E.

··

SOURCES

Einstein: His Life and Universe by Walter Isaacson (Simon & Schuster, 2007)
Albert Einstein: And the Frontiers of Physics by Jeremy Bernstein (Oxford University Press, 1996)
Albert Einstein: Physicist & Genius by Lillian E. Forman (ABDO Publishing, 2009)
Einstein: Visionary Scientist by John B. Severance (Clarion Books, 1999)
Einstein: The Life and Times by Ronald W. Clark (William Morrow, 2007)
Einstein: A Life in Science by Michael White and John Gribbin (Simon & Schuster, 1993)
Einstein: A Biography by Jürgen Neffe (Farrar, Straus and Giroux, 2007)

FURTHER READING FOR KIDS

On a Beam of Light: A Story of Albert Einstein by Jennifer Berne (Chronicle Books, 2013)
Odd Boy Out: Young Albert Einstein by Don Brown (HMH Books, 2008)
Who Was Albert Einstein? by Jess Brallier (Grosset & Dunlap, 2002)
Albert Einstein: The Miracle Mind by Tabatha Yeatts (Sterling, 2007)

··

DIAL BOOKS FOR YOUNG READERS
Published by the Penguin Group • Penguin Group (USA) LLC, 375 Hudson Street, New York, New York 10014

USA | Canada | UK | Ireland | Australia | New Zealand | India | South Africa | China
penguin.com

A PENGUIN RANDOM HOUSE COMPANY

Text copyright © 2014 by Brad Meltzer • Illustrations copyright © 2014 by Christopher Eliopoulos

Library of Congress Cataloging-in-Publication Data
Meltzer, Brad. • I am Albert Einstein / Brad Meltzer ; illustrated by Christopher Eliopoulos.
pages cm • ISBN 978-0-8037-4084-6 (hardcover) • 1. Einstein, Albert, 1879–1955—Pictorial works—Juvenile literature. 2. Physicists—Biography—Juvenile literature. I. Eliopoulos, Christopher, illustrator. II. Title. • QC16.E5M448 2014 530.092—dc23 [B] 2013047226

Photograph on page 37 taken by Sophie Delar. Page 38: Photo of Albert and his sister courtesy of Hulton Archives/Getty Images; photo of Albert in boat courtesy of *New York Times*/Redux. Page 39: Photo of Albert on bicycle courtesy of the Leo Baeck Institute; photo of Albert on his 72nd birthday courtesy of Bettman/CORBIS.

Manufactured in China on acid-free paper • 10 9 8 7 6 5 4 3
Designed by Jason Henry • Text set in Triplex • The artwork for this book was created digitally.

The publisher does not have any control over and does not assume any responsibility for author or third-party websites or their content.

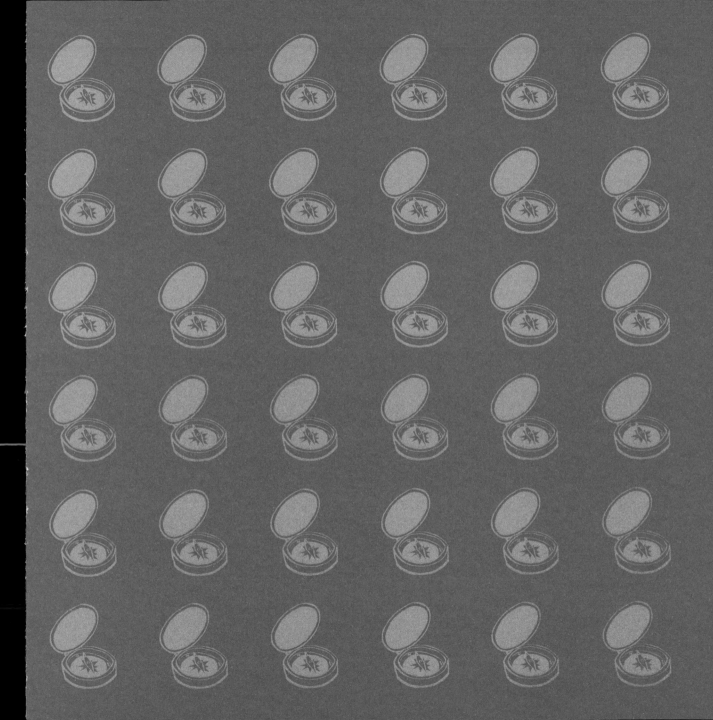

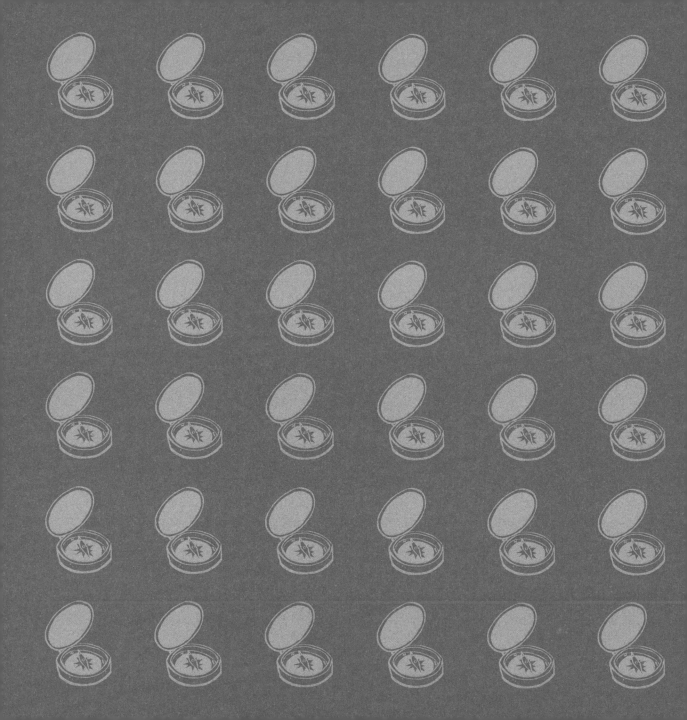